The Sky, the Stars and I

AF624566

Courtenay Scott

BookLeaf Publishing

Presentation by *BookLeaf Publishing*

Web: www.bookleafpub.com

E-mail: info@bookleafpub.com

ISBN: 9789395950268

First edition 2022

This book is dedicated to all the beautiful people in my life who have either come and gone, have passed away, people I have had to let go of, patients, clients, colleagues, my beautiful friends and my family- most of you would know who you are. I believe every single person who I have come across over the past 26 years have been a blessing and I have learnt something from each and every one of you. Thank you for shaping me into the person I am today. How did I get so lucky...

ACKNOWLEDGEMENT

I would like to acknowledge the Gadigal people of the Eora Nation, the traditional custodians of this land and pay my respects to the Elders both past, present and emerging.

PREFACE

From overwhelming gratitude, bliss, adventure and love, to experiences of grief, manipulation and sadness, I always struggled to be vulnerable from a young age. My experiences and relationships shaped and challenged my beliefs about myself, and about the world. But for each and every one of those moments, people and experiences, I am grateful. This is because I have learnt something from them and overtime have come to realise that everything I need exists within me.

Whilst I struggle with vulnerability, I have always used meditation, nature, writing and creativity as a powerful outlet for self expression and realisations. Allowing myself to write what's on my mind freely on paper, or express my true Self through art and connection to nature and the breath, has also brought a deeper awareness of my feelings, thoughts, experiences and have brought to light the not-so-good parts of my personality that I wish to let go of. By doing this, the universe has provided me with profound insights and experiences into the wider world, as well as my true and higher self. I believe that each individual being has the innate ability to do this also.

Publishing this book takes my vulnerability one step further. In sharing my inner thoughts and personal experiences, I hope that it can both help and encourage others to do the same- write, create, be vulnerable, and recognise that there is power in honesty with others and ourselves. Often being honest with those around us can help us to realise that we are not alone. I've recognised that many people go through similar challenges, but it is whether or not we have the courage to step into realness, vulnerability and live authentically that makes a difference.

I have always been a curious person and like to believe that I embrace people without judgement and an open heart. This book was mostly written in the early hours of the morning under the night's sky and stars, where I feel the most grounded, safe, supported, comforted, connected and my mind is clear.

We can learn a lot from other people, as well as nature, culture, animals and the universe and remembering our own inner knowing. This book is my reflection of this.

Privileged

Everyday I am grateful that my career is a
blessing and a privilege.
To continually learn from and be held by
beautiful colleagues and friends
To hold the space for others and their grief
To be with people at their most vulnerable
And to be ok with sitting in silence or
discomfort.
To advocate for those who deserve justice
And to empower people to recognise their
resilience and strengths which have always
existed within them.
To deeply listen
To assist people to feel heard
To help them realise they are not alone
To learn from people older, and younger than me
And to watch other human beings become the
people who they were always meant to be.
Being able to work from a curious mind
A compassionate heart
And a daily sense of gratitude
Is a privilege.

- the blessing as a social worker
1/09/22

Am I still brainwashed?

Yesterday I walked past the bar
And was reminded of the time, yet again, where you had me in your spell.
And took advantage of me
Putting me in positions again, and again which weren't aligned with who I am as a person.

But because of you, I've learnt the importance of assertiveness and being able to say no.
You helped me to understand that powerful anger is only a mask for deep, deep pain.
I am grateful for you.

Sometimes I see you in my dreams
Walking towards me
With sheer rage in your eyes
Even though I know I did nothing wrong.
And I panic.

I haven't seen you in 5 years
But I can still clearly picture your face.
I'm terrified of you.
Which confuses me.
Because I once looked up to you
And you comforted me
Reminding me of the "warrior" that I was.

But never in my life had I felt so scared,
So torn,
So on edge.
And as I reflect back, I know now it was manipulation. But my heart still empathises for you.
I am confused again.
So when I wake up I get a sigh of relief
That you can no longer hurt me.
But can you?
I question myself.

Sometimes I think I see you walking on the streets,
I panic again.
Or wonder if I will ever see you?
And what would I do in that situation?
And I can't talk about it
Because somehow I still believe that even the person I trust the most
Is still wrapped up in your spell.

29/12/20

A Prayer to the Universe

Take away my doubt
And replace it with hope.
Take away my fear
And replace it with trust.
Take all my self criticisms
And fill my body with only love.
Like the sun shines in the season of summer,
Fill my mind, body and soul with radiance.
So that I embrace who I am, and treasure what I have.

27/08/18

I love my friends.

How is friendship so beautiful?
The connection from the Heart that draws two souls together.
It goes beyond the body as a shell
or the value of money or wealth.
Only love
Laughs
Care
Connection
Authenticity
Vulnerability
Spontaneity.
Something that I wasn't used to
Something that I never knew
That I deserved.
From a hurt child
to a sick teen.
She was challenged and scared
In ways that she's still attempting to comprehend.
Maybe that's why I always question-
How is friendship so beautiful?
And how did I get so lucky?
With friends who show me so much love and respect.
That's the reason why everyday I Am Grateful

Blessed
Overwhelmed
That somehow I get to experience love and connection
Without judgment of the external or my past.
And now I Am a strong woman,
Maybe one day I'll remember I Am enough as I Am
And I deserve it all.

03/09/22

Back to the Self

I returned to the city.
High rises
Concrete paths
Too many cars
And the automatic disconnect
From the purposelessness
And presence
Of Nature's Knowing.

Busy
Rushed
Mind
Thoughts
Judgement
Jobs
Comparison
Capitalism
Materialism
Fear.
Falling away from the truth
Of the Self
Of the trees
Of the water
Of the stars
Of the sky
That calls us back to our being.

I am anxious already.
How can I make the effort whilst living in the city, to return to the Self
When the most of world tells me otherwise?

04/09/22

The therapist and her client

I watched you as you cried to me, sobbing.
Tears rolled down your cheeks and you apologised.
Because in this setting, it's supposed to be the other way around.
But as you told me you were proud of me
And told me this is why you do what you do,
We realised that maybe this is how it's supposed to be-
A connection formed over years that is so strong
and grounded in the vulnerability
of both the therapist and her client.

So as you've shared your life with me
and what you've learnt from your challenges
like I have with you,
We talk about how no one is wiser or better than anyone else.
Because we are both humans, continually learning from other beings
and finding resilience from overcoming difficult experiences.
So for me, transformation comes from the trust,
honesty, openness and vulnerability
of both the therapist and her client.

02/01/21

The importance of the present

Am I enjoying the process?
Or am I just rushing into the next “best” thing,
for the next "achievement" or perhaps validation
from others??
But then what?
Is it envy that keeps us going?
With the hope that somehow we’d be like them?
With a love that stays by your side
And a job that says to society you’re
“successful”.
But maybe it’s the safety that we crave?
The false safety that secures the future
And brings calm to the present.
But I've learnt we have no control over what’s
next,
That comparisons aren’t worth my while,
And that envy isn’t worth the exhaustion.
If I live in the future, I'll completely miss this
life all together.
So I let go of comparisons, live in the present,
and enjoy the process.

27/08/18

Progress

Like an old crochet blanket kept in the cupboard
over summer,
She folded away the troubles of the year.
And when it came to winter again, she opened
the cupboard with the blanket inside and was
reminded of her despair from the past.

But that didn't stop her from moving forward.
Instead, she unfolded the blanket of despair,
And draped the past over her bed.
And smiled as she noticed she'd come further
than she realised.

01/03/18

Distance

It makes me kinda sad
How distant we've become
overtime.
That it takes a daughter to come "home"
to an apartment of scattered clothes
and an unfamiliar face
Who later walks through the door
and tells her of the memories that she's made
with him, and her siblings
that she wasn't a part of.

I used to feel bad for not being more intentional
with my time
To see you
And stay with you
And the guilt and sadness only got worse.
Until I realised that there was no effort from you
To see me
To ask me how I was
to ask me to stay
And make more memories with you
Like you do with her

And I know it's unintentional
But it makes me kinda sad

To remember how close we used to be
And how distant we've become overtime.

But maybe someday we'll go to bands,
Run along the beach
and eat dumplings
In an underground bar
Like we used to.
Until one day there'll be no distance
And I'll be asked to make memories with you,
alongside her
overtime.

02/09/22

For Jess

I could see the sadness in your eyes when you talked about her
When you told me about the songs she used to play for you on your way to school,
The photos of her that you keep on your phone,
The way she spoke
And the way she smiled.
You told me once how beautiful I looked
How I looked like an angel
And I reminded you of her.
Whilst you hide away from the sadness with your bright smile,
I can see the love and kindness that she must have brought to the world
Through the love and kindness you showed me.
And I know that she would be so proud of you.
Thank you for all that you've done for me.

19/08/18

What holds us back from being vulnerable?

What if one could break the silence
And they both shared the unspoken with each other
So that she could find a piece of mind,
And somehow she could give her hope
That it's possible to break free from the thoughts that still consume parts of her.
So she could ask more questions of what it's like to have a small piece of freedom.

01/18/18

Love from a daughter

I try to show you through my actions that I
appreciate you.
Because the sadness and anger filled inside me
that I have towards you, somehow won't let me
express that in words.
And though you tell me you don't believe me
or that what I do for you are just forms of
manipulation,
I know my own intentions and I won't stop.
Though you may not accept it, I will always love
you more than you know.

20/08/18

not okay.

You took what you could from me.
My childhood, innocence, my confidence and
love.
And you threw it away because I was nothing to
you
But a body
Left cold in the middle of a paddock.
Though you never actually got to know me
and you thought I would forget,
I haven't.
and it makes me sad that you probably wouldn't
remember
The day you changed my life.

24/08/18

Eyes

The depth of a person's eyes
can reveal so much about them
-their sadness, fear, love, chemistry, joy,
judgement, stress, loneliness.

Whilst the blue mask covers your face,
your eyes still tell the story of yourSelf.

And like I see through your eyes how your soul
holds so much pain,
I hope you see how my eyes show so much love
and compassion for you-
Because I care about you and will do my best to
help you.

Through the depth of our eyes, a beautiful
connection was made.

Always learning

I learnt that you can't make someone change.
Nor can you rely on the "best" external help to
shift your thinking.
Change can only come from you.
Let go of blaming others for not giving you what
you need,
Let go of being the victim
and take responsibility for your life by owning
your own reality.
Your relationship to yourSelf will remain with
you forever and beyond.
Work on that.
Learn to be ok on your own. Because you are
never lonely.
Can we trust ourselves, be supported by the
breath, and allow support from others who can
only guide us back to the strength that exists
within ourselves.

05/12/20

Open my heart

I was scared to be vulnerable
To be in a relationship
Because I didn't want to be hurt again.
I didn't want the past to come rushing back
And remind me of all the times that I was
mistreated.
Now I'm afraid it's too late.
When I see you move on
And notice how the past has kept me stuck.
So I hold onto the hope that someday I'll find
someone.
That one day I'll be vulnerable enough
To let someone in,
Open my heart,
And remember I Am capable of being loved.

04/01/21

I Am

"So Hum" she meditated.
As she lay in savasana,
After acknowledging her yoga practice
And all that her body has brought her through.
"I am that
I am all.
All that is within me
All that guides and protects me".

A tear falls down her cheek.
Because within, she is grateful
For her life
Her resilience
Her strength
Her well being
How strong her body is,
Her heart.
Despite all she has put it through.
So hum (I am).

04/12/20

Another 3am morning

My body wakes at 3am
To be grounded by the sky
To see my loved ones in the stars
To write under the moon
To find solitude in the sounds of nature.

Clear thoughts
Open heart.
Fresh mind.
Pen to paper.

Beneath a constructed personality-
judgement, comparison, jealousy, materialism, capitalism.
Shaped by fear-based values,
I unravel the layers
Unveil the knowing of the Heart
And return to the Self which is love
- The only thing that is real.

Another 3am morning.
Clear thoughts
Open heart.
Fresh mind.
Pen to paper.

Where is my mind?
You're in my mind.

Your strength
Your smile
Your hugs
Your generosity
Your eyes
Your stories.

Where is my heart?
You're in my heart.
Forever and always, Pa.

06/09/22

Life is beautiful

She could not walk
Now she can
She could not think
Now she can
She could not speak
Now she can
She could not rest
Now she can
She could not recognise the world's beauty
Now she can
They thought she would not wake up
But then she did.
I once lost most of myself
But then somehow saved myself all at once.

And I am grateful for her every single day.

12/12/19

Less Disconnected

The birds they speak
The animals they play
The ocean it heals
The trees they teach
The earth it grounds
The children we learn from.
As adults we crave connection
To what we think is from other humans
But have become disconnected from the rest.

Who are we to think we are as wiser and more
powerful than the children, nature, the animals?
We are all connected, all equal, all the same.

As adults, can we be more like the children?
More aware
More connected
More honest
More loving
More innocent
More curious
More playful
Less anxious
Less judgemental
Less exposure
Less disconnected.
6/9/22

A smile

Yesterday I saw a person on the street
That reminded me of you.
With blue hair, a black jumper and the same
smile I used to see sitting beside me on the
couch each morning.
And the grief never leaves
The sadness never goes
But the peace extends
Within me everyday
Knowing that your still here
With a smile in the sky
Watching me through the stars.

20/08/18

www.ingramcontent.com/pod-product-compliance
Lightning Source LLC
Chambersburg PA
CBHW051753130826
49812CB00033B/1125
9789395950268